T0099514

Empowering the

Public-Private Partnership

Empowering the Public-Private Partnership

The Future of America's Local Government

George V. Voinovich

Introduction by
R. Gregory Browning and Hunter Morrison

Afterword by Hunter Morrison

Ohio University Press in association with the
Voinovich School of Leadership and Public Affairs

Athens, Ohio

Ohio University Press, Athens, Ohio 45701
ohioswallow.com
© 2017 by Ohio University Press
All rights reserved

To obtain permission to quote, reprint, or
otherwise reproduce or distribute material from
Ohio University Press publications, please contact
our rights and permissions department at
(740) 593-1154 or (740) 593-4536 (fax).

Frontispiece: George V. Voinovich, 2008. *U.S. government photo*

Printed in the United States of America
Ohio University Press books are printed on acid-free paper ⊗ ™

27 26 25 24 23 22 21 20 19 18 17   5 4 3 2 1

Library of Congress Control Number: 2017942363

contents

CONTENTS

acknowledgment

Ohio University's Voinovich School of Leadership and Public Affairs was honored to assist Senator George Voinovich and the Ohio University Press in reviewing and finalizing this manuscript. Mike Zimmer, an executive in residence, and G. Jason Jolley, an associate professor with the Voinovich School of Leadership and Public Affairs, served as reviewers for the book and provided helpful suggestions to Senator Voinovich and Ohio University Press.

George V. Voinovich and Janet Voinovich, June 19, 2010.
By permission of the Ohio Republican Party

Empowering the

Public-Private Partnership

introduction

R. *Gregory Browning and Hunter Morrison*

George Voinovich was a practical man, and this book is a primer for practitioners. Written in plain language, it is a handbook of best practices for elected and appointed officials and for leaders from the private and philanthropic sectors who partner with them for the betterment of their community. His words here distill the knowledge and wisdom of a man who dedicated his career to public service at the local, state, and federal levels and who was, as a result, a person uniquely qualified to reflect on the qualities of civic leadership required to get things done.

Voinovich was passionate about the power of public-private partnerships (P3s) to transform a community. He was widely respected for his honesty, authenticity, and straight talk, so you can believe him when he says that these partnerships will work for you—because he tried them himself in his positions as mayor and governor. In this primer, he describes the critical steps to follow when building any partnership and tells the story of how the practice of partnering unfolded in the City of Cleveland and the State of Ohio under his stewardship.

Voinovich was a storyteller. But unlike those who delight in telling stories that reflect well on themselves, he'd tell stories about the people who joined him in the efforts to rebuild Cleveland after years of contentious political infighting and later to set the State of Ohio on a fiscally sound trajectory. Voinovich campaigned for mayor of Cleveland on the slogan "Together We Can Do It." This primer is about how "together we did it." Here he tells stories about the individuals and organizations he brought together to advance their common interest in the community whose history and future they shared.

Voinovich saw community as a dynamic, interactive system that performs best when its leaders adhere to rules of civility and value the interests and humanity of each person with whom and for whom they work. He summed up this complex process in one word: symbiosis. Drawn from the world of biology, it describes an interdependent or mutually beneficial relationship between two or more organisms. He delighted in dropping "symbiosis" into the middle of otherwise mundane remarks at a ground breaking or ribbon cutting and then telling his audience that the project they were gathered together to celebrate was a perfect example of how people could accomplish great things by working together. This primer is filled with stories about the ways in which he engaged parties with seemingly disparate interests, encouraged them to find their mutual goals, and urged them to collaborate for the common good. These stories suggest how you, too, can encourage the symbiotic civic relationships that will foster long-term success in your community.

Voinovich was a teacher who practiced civic pedagogy everywhere he went. He taught several generations of public servants how to work together to "do more with less" and "work harder and smarter." He believed that the art of public leadership requires establishing clear, easily understood goals, communicating them relentlessly, and monitoring them consistently. He had no patience with cynical indifference, bureaucratic infighting, or empire building. This primer tells how he and his chief of staff, Tom Wagner, used Cleveland's Operations Improvement Task Force (OITF) to engage city staff in creating a practical plan for improving operations and then to hold those staff accountable for carrying out their own recommendations.

Voinovich respected the intelligence and dedication of those who choose to make a career in public service. He believed that the vast majority want more than just "to do their job and collect a paycheck." They want to improve the lives of their fellow citizens. He believed that many public servants have an untapped desire to work beyond the limits of their job description to make a real difference in their community. The OITF brought these desires to the surface and channeled them into specific initiatives that have made a difference for Cleveland and its citizens. This primer tells of how he took the lessons learned from the OITF and applied them statewide though a disciplined system of Total Quality Management (TQM). He believed that the lessons of civic collaboration are scalable and can improve performance at every level of government.

Finally, Voinovich was a leader. Modest and unassuming, he avoided grand promises and high-sounding rhetoric. He preferred, instead, to speak about practical accomplishments and the important role that others played in making those accomplishments possible. At his core, he was a leader committed to putting good ideas to work for the benefit of the communities he served. He firmly believed that those privileged to lead a government, a corporation, a university, or a philanthropy have an obligation to serve interests beyond their own. Not unremarkably, he found that when asked, most of those in leadership positions responded positively—if they could be assured that their contribution would be valued and effective. He believed that one of his roles as a public leader was to make good on that promise. By valuing and celebrating the accomplishments of others, he restored civility and trust to Cleveland's civic life and established a virtuous cycle of public and private reinvestment that has fueled several decades of increasingly sophisticated development initiatives in the city's downtown and its neighborhoods.

Voinovich wrote this primer about P3s as a practical tool for meeting the challenges of public management in a world of straitened circumstances. The lessons that he learned during his ten years as Cleveland's mayor and eight years as Ohio's governor are even more relevant today than they were in years past. When he was sworn in as Cleveland's fifty-fourth mayor in 1980, constrained municipal resources were more the exception than the rule for local governments. Today they are more the rule than the exception. He tells how, in the face of the city's dire economic conditions, he turned to Cleveland's business and philanthropic communities for help—first in analyzing the city's finances, operations, and economic prospects, and then in taking concrete steps to address together the challenges they found.

Chapter 1 lays out those challenges that Voinovich faced when he took the helm as mayor in November 1980 following two years of municipal chaos, conflict between city government and the local business community, corrosive racial strife, neighborhood disinvestment in the face of court-ordered school busing and accelerating white flight, and growing economic hardship as the first wave of deindustrialization hit Cleveland's factories and the neighborhoods that surrounded them.

This chapter goes on to describe the process of developing the city's first P3—the OITF—which laid the groundwork for other partnerships to follow. Hidden within the accounts of specific actors and their contributions is a powerful lesson about the value of beginning any collaboration with an honest and detailed analysis of the facts on the ground. Voinovich takes up this theme and continues to explore it in subsequent chapters, in which he describes his efforts to sustain the involvement of the business community in the work of city government and to encourage local foundations to invest in improving city operations and developing catalytic downtown and neighborhood projects. Simply put, he learned that when business and foundation leaders are actively involved from day one in identifying and analyzing a problem, they are more likely to invest in addressing and solving that problem in the months and years that follow.

Finally, he argues that a community's infrastructure of human relations is more important than its visible, physical infrastructure. He believed that Cleveland's leadership had to deal honestly and directly with the city's underlying racial tensions before it could hope to build successful partnerships, and he describes the Cleveland Roundtable, a P3 created expressly to redress the persistent inequities that had fed anger and mistrust and had stymied the city's progress for several decades.

Chapter 2 describes in detail the process he used to put P3s to work in Cleveland through the OITF. It should be read not just as a war story about how Cleveland began its decades-long recovery but also as a case study about the practical aspects of partnering at a municipal or state level. To this end, he details the steps he took and the lessons he learned in creating and sustaining the OITF. This checklist is a practical tool for taking the first step toward a municipal P3— establishing an operations improvement task force to engage civic leaders and public servants in defining and analyzing the challenges the city faces and beginning a disciplined process of addressing them one by one.

Chapter 3 speaks to an important initiative that paralleled the OITF: the audit. Voinovich details the dire financial condition in which he found the city and the steps he took to engage both state officials and local business leaders in finding a way out of the fiscal mess he inherited. While Cleveland's fiscal condition in 1980 was extreme, the realities of municipal fiscal stress are not uncommon today. This chapter once again makes the case for engaging local business leadership, as well as state and federal officials, in finding ways in which your city can "do more with less" and deliver basic services while operating within its means.

Voinovich recognized that in a democracy, power and responsibility are shared. Chapter 4 speaks to how he engaged his political competitors, local unions, and civil servants in making quality everyone's business. Every city has a complex mix of organizations and individuals whose interests must somehow be addressed if progress is to be made. Voinovich tells how he engaged Cleveland's powerful city council president, George Forbes, as a full partner in the city's recovery and shared the credit for work they did together. He relates the importance of involving union leadership and respecting the work of union members in the life of the city. And finally, he emphasizes the value of engaging the city's employees as full participants in the city's recovery. In so doing, he unleashed the creativity and enthusiasm of dedicated public servants whose contributions had too often been overlooked by prior administrations.

This chapter also shows how Voinovich used the experience of implementing Cleveland's OITF to adapt and improve the method at the state level when he became governor in 1991. By that time, many of the same principles and practices that he and his public- and private-sector partners had worked out on their own had been systematized and were going by a new name: Total Quality Management.

Chapter 5 addresses the challenge of sustaining civic participation in the work of the city. Voinovich believed that too often, members of blue-ribbon committees like the OITF do their work, issue their report, and then return to their day jobs. He believed that it was critical to the city's long-term future that the enthusiasm of these civic volunteers be sustained for the months and years that it would take to bring about real change in the way the city did its business. To that end, he created the Mayor's Operation Volunteer Effort (MOVE). This multifaceted initiative established a volunteer program to continue bringing loaned executives into city departments, convened a public relations advisory board to address the city's poor national image, and established the annual Mayor's Award for Volunteerism to thank volunteers for their work and give them the recognition they richly deserved. Finally, he discusses how he applied the lessons he learned through Cleveland's OITF to the State of Ohio, instituting TQM and encouraging the state's business leaders to institutionalize their own civic engagement by establishing the Ohio Business Roundtable.

In chapter 6, Voinovich identifies a fourth "P" that has played a critical and continuing role in the city's sustained recovery: local philanthropy. Cleveland is blessed with multiple local foundations and a generations-long history of philanthropic investment in the city. He details the important roles that local philanthropies—the Cleveland Foundation and the George Gund Foundation in particular—played in the city's recovery by supporting baseline studies on municipal operations, finances, and infrastructure; providing significant funding for the OITF; and leading the effort to implement the OITF through targeted investments in staff training, critical personnel initiatives, land information systems, and other innovations for which scarce tax dollars were unavailable. Voinovich writes with obvious pride of the partnership's success in encouraging the foundations, businesses, and civic leaders to invest in two of the city's most successful downtown development projects: the Cleveland lakefront, home of the Rock and Roll Hall of Fame and the Great Lakes Science Center; and Playhouse Square, the nation's second-largest theater complex.

This chapter is important not just for its recounting of the catalytic role that philanthropy has played in Cleveland. Voinovich wrote it in the hope that he could encourage other communities to engage their own philanthropies in the work of their city. He firmly believed that civic partnering is everyone's business and that no organization or individual who cared about their community could be left on the sidelines watching the game. In his roles as mayor and governor, he did everything he could to encourage everyone to get in the game.

Finally, Voinovich was a civic entrepreneur who understood instinctively that in order to accomplish great things, a community must develop trust among its members and build a record of success through collaboration to replace a history of frustration and conflict. He accomplished this by bringing together all of the parties who had an interest in pursuing a big idea and then relentlessly challenging them to "do the doable." He began with the OITF, an initiative that bore long-term results. By focusing first on achieving basic operational improvements in city government, he and his team built the skills, credibility, and relationships of trust, both within and outside city hall, that enabled the city to pursue increasingly complex projects. Simply put, he believed that by beginning at the beginning with an operations improvement task force, a new mayor or governor can build a network of P3s that can tackle the difficult challenges they face.

Voinovich did not write this primer as a biography celebrating his considerable successes as a public leader. That, he believed, would be for others to do. He wrote it for the leaders of today and tomorrow who, as he was, are confronted with the challenge of doing the public's work in the face of economic uncertainty and severely constrained resources. He believed that "together we can do it" and daily put that mantra to work in a public career that spanned five decades and earned him the reputation as the most successful public leader in Ohio's history. He wrote this primer in the hope that by applying his hard-won lessons, you, the reader, might navigate with greater certainty the uncharted waters of public service in the months and years ahead.

one

Why We Did It

You might wonder why, at this late stage in life, someone who has been a state representative, county auditor, county commissioner, lieutenant governor, mayor, governor, and senator would be writing a handbook on public-private partnerships (P3s). The reason is simple: I want to continue to make a difference for my country, and I truly believe that this handbook will help improve the management of cities and towns across America and enhance the quality of life of their residents.

My belief in the P3, which in general terms is an outcome-based collaboration between local government and business, has not changed over my forty-four years of government service or four years of "retirement." As I once put it, "Successful local economic development and management of cities . . . will largely depend on a community's ability to foster effective public private partnerships."[1] I still believe that, and I'm not the only one.

In addition, this book is a case study of Cleveland's Operations Improvement Task Force (OITF), the P3 that helped turn the city around in the 1980s when I was mayor. It also presents an overview of the related Total Quality Management (TQM) and continuous improvement program that I implemented at the state level in the early 1990s when I was governor. It is a how-to manual that will not only explain the technical aspects of creating a P3 but also describe how the private sector can be a powerful agent in improving the operations of local government. It sets forth how the Cleveland task force was created; what motivated those who gave of their time, talent, and money; and how the partners monitored the implementation of its recommendations.

Moreover, the book will demonstrate how this joint endeavor improved city government, fostered a decades-long partnership between the city and private sector, and spawned other collaborative projects that continue to this day. It tells the story of how Cleveland was saved—and believe me, "saved" is not an overstatement.

Some might argue that the federal and state governments can and must do more to help local governments financially. Experience, however, shows that they are mistaken. The best that realistically can be hoped for is to maintain those state and federal programs that make a difference in our cities, such as community development block grants, the low-income housing tax credit, and the new markets tax credit. But the future of these programs remains in jeopardy because of our country's unsustainable debt situation.

Trends in state government policy have exacerbated the difficulties facing local governments. I recall a speech that I gave at the National League of Cities convention in 1981, when I was mayor. I noted that a number of governors, when talking about state and local control, made the words "local government" sound almost like a slur.

In 1981, when President Ronald Reagan organized the New Federalism Task Force to affirm the primacy of the Tenth Amendment authority of the states over that of the federal government regarding local issues, I pointed out that the reason why so many cities were coming to the federal government with a tin cup was that their states gave them no ability to raise revenues on the local level. I suggested that President Reagan call a meeting of governors to urge them to provide the revenue vehicles necessary for local governments to meet their responsibilities. My belief was, and is, that dollars raised locally are the best-spent dollars—and even better, they do not include the brokerage fees collected by the federal government.

These political and economic contexts are powerful and must be addressed on multiple levels. P3s, while not the solution to every problem, can do much to help state and local governments navigate their way toward outcomes that better address citizen needs, including job creation and economic growth. This is the central subject of this handbook, and the story begins with the first formal P3 that I helped create, the OITF in Cleveland. I have always taken a pragmatic approach to problem solving, and the P3 is a powerful tool.

The need for such an approach has intensified in the intervening years. The growing public frustration with Washington, and, in some cases, with state capitals, has increased both the need and the desire for action on the local level. And even though corporations of all sizes are leaner than they were thirty-five years ago, I'm confident that they are still as ready to get into the arena with local government as were corporate leaders in Cleveland in the 1980s. In his journal article "Business Leadership Lessons from the Cleveland Turnaround," James E. Austin captured what happened in that place and time: "A relatively small group of Cleveland business and civic leaders stepped forward after the bankruptcy to move the community in new directions. Among these were the CEOs of the city's biggest corporations who were clearly recognized as the informal leaders of the local business community. Together, these leaders, through 'personal selling,' were able to convince their colleagues at other major companies of the imperative of action."[2]

There's another resource to be tapped, as well: citizen volunteers. As people live longer and, in some cases, retire earlier, many are looking for an opportunity to use their talent, time, energy, and experience to make a difference in their community. They have been joined by a generation of millennials who are interested in urban affairs and are looking for ways to contribute. And there are people like Ed Richard, my executive assistant when I was mayor, who left his successful private business to work in government because of a similar motivation. His business background and experience turned out to be indispensable to improving Cleveland during his ten years in my administration.

I'd known Ed for several years before then. He was the founder of the Council of Small Enterprises, a group of small businessmen who became part of our chamber of commerce. Ed said that he wanted to be one of my advisers, and I replied, "I don't have advisers, but I'd be grateful if you joined my administration." And he did. When I later asked him why, he said, "It's rather simple. I had reached the stage in my career where I felt I was just coasting. . . . I really did not feel challenged, and making money alone was not my reason for being in business. So when this opportunity just hit me in the face, I said 'Yes' without thinking. It was a good decision because one can really make a difference in city government, and I felt I was doing that."[3]

As Ed's words convey, there are still people in America who believe in Abraham Lincoln's definition of government: "The legitimate object of government is to do for a community of people whatever they need to have done, but cannot do at all, or cannot so well do, for themselves, in their separate and individual capacities. In all that the people can individually do as well for themselves, government ought not to interfere."⁴ And I would add this: the community should not wait for the government but instead should join with it to achieve those goals. The government is just one thread in the fabric of the community, and I believe that a leader's highest calling is to empower people and channel their energy and resources to help solve problems, meet challenges, and seize opportunities.

I also believe that it is a leader's role to reach deep into every individual, draw out the goodness that's inside, and inspire them to use it to help their families, their neighbors, and their communities.

So I have decided that with the time I have left, I want to do all I can to promote P3s, which, as this handbook will show, are among the most practical, efficient, and effective ways to improve the quality of life for our citizens, whether they live in large cities, suburban enclaves, or small towns.

When local governments have a new executive or new council members, it's a good time to revisit city operations, just as a company would review its corporate operations under new leadership to determine whether it is doing its efficient best for its shareholders.

So how do you start? A successful P3 begins with the recognition of a need by both public and private sectors. Businesses, nonprofits, and foundations must be ready to respond to a call for help from the public sector, or they may take the initiative and express their willingness to help by providing human capital and, possibly, financial resources. Similarly, when need arises, public officials must reach out for help or respond positively when an offer from the private sector presents itself. I have observed that too often, public leaders do not understand what a fantastic resource they have in the private sector, and that on the private side, businesses can be reluctant to get involved in the politics of city governance. Citizens may believe that corporate action is about only corporate interests, as opposed to the public interest. These potential causes of misunderstanding underscore the need for openness and transparency from both public and private actors.

The Genesis of the Cleveland Public-Private Partnerships

Let's recall what Cleveland was like in 1979. The comedian Rich Little made Cleveland the butt of jokes in his stand-up routine. Johnny Carson, host of *The Tonight Show*, took a poke at our city by saying, "Will the last person leaving Cleveland please turn off the lights?" That was when Cleveland was known as the town where the river burned and the mayor's hair caught fire.

But joking aside, Cleveland did have severe problems. In 1978, Cleveland became the first city since the Great Depression to go into fiscal default after declaring that it could not pay off $15 million in short-term notes held by local banks.[5] Later, the State of Ohio declared that the city's finances were unauditable.

How did it come to that?

As is usually the case, it wasn't any one thing but a combination of many that had created this dire situation. Years of financial mismanagement were followed by the use of one-time revenues, such as the proceeds from the sale of the sewer system to the regional sewer district for $32 million in 1972 and the sale of the municipal transit system to a regional transit authority for $8.9 million two years later. A paper contracted through the Brookings Institution concluded that Cleveland was a virtual ward of the federal government because it received $100 million annually, almost as much as the city collected in property and income taxes.[6]

The city's infrastructure had deteriorated, as roads, bridges, sewers, and water lines buckled and crumbled. Some suburbs were suing to take control of the city's water system and incorporate it into a regional system. Unemployment was high, and litter lay strewn about the streets.

On top of that, the city was unable to obtain credit, in part because it had not been paying its bills to vendors. As Ed Richard described it, "We entered City Hall, and it was a mess. . . . I was in my new office with the door closed. There was a banging on my door. I yelled through the door, 'Who is it?' The response was 'I'm Tom Whelan of Ohio Bell. You owe us $300,000 for phone service, and we'll be shutting off your phones next week unless you pay.' It seems the prior administration had not paid many bills, including telephone for several months. We later found bills stuffed into filing cabinets, along with checks that had never been deposited."[7]

Cleveland also had a bloated thirty-three-member city council, one of the largest in the nation. The mayor and council members served terms of only two years, so divisive elections were ongoing. There was more of a focus on running for or staying in office than on effectively serving in that office.

Mayor Dennis Kucinich and the Cleveland City Council were at war with one another. The mayor spent a good deal of time announcing what he was against rather than what he was for, and the result was constant strife. In fact, the division was so pronounced that a recall election was held, which the mayor survived by only 236 votes out of a total of 120,300 cast.

After I became mayor, with the help of such organizations as the Citizens League and the League of Women Voters, we made two crucial changes in the structure of city government. The citizens of Cleveland voted to reduce the size of city council from thirty-three to twenty-one members, and they extended the term of office for both the mayor and the council to four years, beginning with the next election. The changes were significant, but they addressed only a few of the many ills that afflicted the community.

Minority residents were angry with the police department, both for the slow response to their calls for help and for what they (often correctly) perceived as the use of excessive force by police officers. This lack of trust between the city's police department and its citizens lingered long after the race riots of 1968. The constantly changing leadership of the police force also reflected the turmoil in city law enforcement: Cleveland had thirteen police chiefs in the seventeen years leading up to 1979. Police officers had their own justified complaints about resources—they pointed out, for example, that 80 percent of the city's police cars had more than one hundred thousand miles on them. The fire department was little better off, as the Vanguards Organization, which represented African American firefighters, was suing the city for racial discrimination within the department.

I knew that unless we dealt with the racial tensions, the chance of bringing the community together to build P3s was nonexistent. So we created the Cleveland Roundtable, which brought together leaders from every group in the city, including neighborhood and religious organizations. It took on the jobs of dealing with racism; discrimination in housing, employment, and education; and public anger over the issue of federal court-ordered school busing.

We were fortunate that the business community understood, as I did, that the infrastructure of human relations was more important than our physical infrastructure.

I knew that the community had great assets and was a national leader in the arts, education, health care, community involvement, and philanthropy. I also was aware of the number of large corporations headquartered in the city—TRW, British Petroleum, and Eaton, for example—along with two large

philanthropic organizations, the Cleveland Foundation and the George Gund Foundation. Having
served in elected office at both the state and the local
levels, I knew many of these corporate and foundation leaders personally, and I was convinced that if I
could get them involved in improving how the city
was managed, we would have the talent and other resources to be successful.

As a former county auditor, I was familiar with
management audits. In fact, the first management audit
of a county office had taken place on my watch and
had resulted in a dramatic change in its operations.
The result was a marked improvement in the delivery
of services to the public. There was no question in my
mind that the city also needed a massive management
audit to bring about the same sort of changes that
we had made in the county auditor's office. In addition, I knew that the management audit conducted by
Warren King & Associates in 1963 for the Ohio state
government had produced such good results that then-
governor Ronald Reagan hired them to do the same in
California.

I also understood the need to recruit outstanding
talent to run the city's departments. I was confident
that those participating in the OITF would work with
me to attract the finest talent and identify outstanding
people already in city government.

The morning after I won the election, I was on
the phone with the Cleveland and Gund Foundations. Both had been briefed on the proposed OITF

and had agreed to help finance it, but only on the condition that the private sector would match their funding, dollar for dollar. I met that same day with E. Mandell "Del" de Windt, the chairman of Eaton and de facto spokesman for the business community. He told me that the private sector would match the $250,000 provided by the two foundations. In fact, they even exceeded that goal: more than $550,000 was raised from three hundred contributors, including eight labor unions and a cross section of the community that I never anticipated would help. Morton Mandel, then the CEO of Premier Industrial, was a leader in the fund-raising. He later said, "Five or six of us took 30 names, and divided them up among us. . . . It was the easiest fundraising of this importance I had ever done."[8]

The OITF was a giant success; it helped get Cleveland's finances on solid ground and improved the efficiency of city government. The Department of Community Development reorganized its operations to take better advantage of Housing and Urban Development grants, and that change resulted in a 100 percent increase in grants directly supporting Cleveland's neighborhoods.

By 1982, the OITF recommendations had saved $4 million by streamlining operations in the fire department and waste collection department alone. The city established an Office of Internal Audit, and Cleveland's bond rating increased from an abysmal Ca1 in 1978 to Aaa in 1996. Just two years after the OITF's creation, 94 percent of the recommendations had been implemented or were in progress, and they had resulted in $30 million in savings each year.

The Genesis of This Book

And that is how I come to this handbook, a how-to manual and leadership guide that outlines the philosophy and the technical aspects of creating an effective P3. It will explain how to persuade the private sector to get involved and will show how I worked with business leaders to motivate others to provide the people and money that we needed for the task force and to implement its recommendations. It also will examine the impact of the recommendations in improving government operations.

My first goal is to inspire readers to consider creating a P3 in their own communities. My second goal is to provide a playbook that can be used to implement the systemic managerial changes that can and will improve how local government performs and delivers. The lessons conveyed through this work will underscore the symbiotic relationship between the public and private sectors of nearly every town in America.

As former Cleveland City Council president Jay Westbrook has said, "Most of us realize that very little of what we can do lies in legislation. There are very few laws that you can pass at a municipal level to hold families together, get people jobs, or maintain a quality of life in the neighborhoods. This has really compelled us to develop alliances and build bridges with other organizations."[9]

Those who are moved to learn more after reading this handbook will be happy to know that original materials documenting the OITF that are not included in this handbook can be found within the vast written materials, correspondence, and official papers of the Voinovich Collections, open and available to all. The archives comprise four collections, which Cleveland State University, Ohio University, and the Western Reserve Historical Society are digitizing thanks to a grant from the Cleveland Foundation.

Why is all this important now? As I said earlier, little or no help will be forthcoming from the federal or state government, and I believe that the situation of local governments will only get worse. As I look around the country, I am extremely concerned that many of the fiscal, operational, and human relations challenges that I worked through in the 1980s as mayor and in the 1990s as governor are the same challenges facing cities and states today. Municipal bankruptcy, fiscal emergencies, and race relations are but a few examples. It is, as Yogi Berra said, "déjà vu all over again."

Here's a silver lining though: today, there are tools and templates for elected officials, businesses, labor organizations, organized philanthropies, and nonprofits to make use of their limited financial and human capital to meet challenges, solve problems, and take advantage of undiscovered opportunities. These tools were used effectively in Cleveland, and they exist in every community in America.

My slogan when I ran in the mayoral election in 1979 was "Together We Can Do It." But it was more than that. It was a statement of what I truly believed.

And I know it works, because we did it.

two

The Cleveland Operations Improvement Task Force

The success of the Operations Improvement Task Force is due in great part to three people who played integral roles: E. Mandell "Del" de Windt, the chairman of Eaton and the representative of the business community with whom I worked most closely; Jack Hushen, Eaton's manager of public affairs, whom Del appointed executive director of the OITF steering committee; and Ben Bryan, Jack's public-sector counterpart and implementation coordinator for the OITF. In this chapter, I have drawn on their perspectives on all the important components of an effective P3.

This chapter draws on correspondence and other contributions from E. Mandell de Windt, Jack Hushen, and Ben Bryan.

As I described in chapter 1, when we began, the city's finances were declared unauditable by the State of Ohio, and the city could not pay $15 million in notes called in by local banks. Cleveland had gone into default and was essentially a ward of the federal government. Its infrastructure was deteriorating, with roads, bridges, sewers, and water lines buckling and crumbling. The city was unable to obtain credit because it had not been paying its bills to vendors. There was an overwhelming feeling among Cleveland's business leaders that something had to be done quickly to get the city off its downward spiral and onto an upward track. The situation was critical.

Foundations for a Successful P3

I had an important advantage even before I became mayor: *personal relationships* built over many years. Many leaders in the business community had been frustrated by elected officials, especially those at Cleveland City Hall, who had considered them adversaries. So when they urged me to run for mayor, they assured me that they would step forward to assist should I be elected. These were people I knew and trusted and with whom I had worked before when I held public office in Cuyahoga County. Their pledge of support was what helped me decide to run. We agreed that the future of our city depended to a large extent on the involvement of business and that no one sector of society can go it alone. The private sector can't, local government can't, and neither can unions or nonprofits.

When developing a P3, one of the first steps that a local government executive—whether mayor or city manager—must take is to *ask for help* in solving the city's problems.

Another is to *establish trust*. Like many big cities at the time, Cleveland had been studied to death. Each study ended with a thick, spiral-bound notebook and little or no action. Businesses do not run on pretty pictures and multicolored charts. They run on results. The private sector will not commit time and resources to a P3 unless assured that it will result in action rather than rhetoric. I made a pledge that I would personally back the recommendations of the OITF and participate in their implementation. Without the commitment of a chief executive officer to carry out—not just talk about—change, I doubt that any such initiative will succeed. Only when a level of trust has been established can the public and private halves of the partnership begin to work together.

The next step is to secure the *resources* needed to begin the project. Cleveland commissioned a private consulting firm to propose a program and a plan of action to bring modern management techniques to the city, streamline the administration of government, and eliminate duplication and overlap. The ensuing proposal was keyed to extensive participation by the private sector. The business community would have to help recruit the *people* and raise the *money* needed to get the job done. The consultants could act as advisers, but the studies, recommendations, and implementation would have to be carried out by a task force of committed partners.

Smart business owners and managers know that the success of their companies is tied to their communities and to the quality of life of their workers, and if they don't know it, you should lay it out for them as plainly and persuasively as you can. Call it the principle of enlightened self-interest. You should look also to individuals who sit on the boards of charitable or nonprofit organizations; they will have experience in persuading others to respond to the needs of a cause.

In Cleveland, we established an *executive committee* of top-level corporate officers from major firms in the city, much like a board of directors. We also assembled a *ways and means committee* and gave its members the job of securing pledges for people and money.

The response in Cleveland was quick and dramatic: ninety men and women of exceptional talent—$3 million worth of exceptional talent, in fact—volunteered for task force duty. Employers were willing to *loan employees*, among their most skilled, to work on the task force. Two Cleveland foundations underwrote a $250,000 challenge grant that was matched with contributions from more than 250 companies of all sizes. Organized labor, as well as church and community development organizations, made substantial contributions. In all, more than $800,000 was raised.

Another key to success in any P3 is *communication*. It is important that each partner have a point person who acts as a clear channel to the others. In Cleveland, we were lucky to have Del de Windt, for example, as representative of the business community. Without him and others like him, we would not have had the OITF and many of the other P3s that resulted from it. Each partner in the shared enterprise should be represented by a trusted and reliable spokesperson. And always say what you mean and mean what you say.

Organization

The OITF was designed to report and recommend methods for achieving more efficient and cost-effective operations of city government. But first, we had to *organize*. This took place in three distinct phases:

1. A four-week period to get prepared, funded, and staffed

2. A twelve-week full-time effort to document, study, and evaluate the problems and to propose solutions

3. The integration and editing of an approved report

Working in partnership requires *coordination*. Del de Windt appointed Eaton's director of public affairs, Jack Hushen, as executive director of a task force steering committee for the private-sector partners. It was his job to make sure that things stayed on track and that all the corporate partners honored their responsibilities.

The loaned executives had to be real leaders—people whose skills and services would be difficult to replace—not just tokens or, worse yet, dead weight. Del's and Jack's insistence on this level of quality made all the difference in the success of the program.

Ben Bryan was Jack's counterpart in the public sector. Ben worked with the City of Cleveland as the implementation coordinator of the OITF for five years. The first two years were as the private-sector liaison for the study, a position through which he developed the task force's recommendations and the plan for their implementation. For the next three years, he was on the city's payroll, charged with working with my chief of staff to implement the recommendations and other associated tasks.

The volunteer loaned executives formed four teams, each headed by an expert in the discipline involved. The number of teams and the areas of expertise of the volunteers must be tailored to the specific needs of your P3. Finding the *right people* for the *right job* is tremendously important. If you don't know or are unsure, by all means, ask for advice.

Some task force members began their work with a degree of apprehension. They soon lost their reservations, however, and plunged in with an eagerness to get more involved. They found that most city employees were dedicated and hard-working people who were more than willing to cooperate, and they also came to appreciate the unique problems of governing and managing a large city. Working together on the

OITF fostered *professional relationships* and respect between the loaned private-sector executives and their
city counterparts. I've stayed in touch with many
participants from this and other partnerships, and I've
heard them say that what they accomplished through
the OITF was a highlight of their professional careers.
Most also noted that they could not have done it without support from the people they worked with at their
own offices.

Once the teams were in place, they began studying
the multitude of departments in Cleveland's city government, grouping them into four general categories:

- Public properties and public service

- Public safety

- Public utilities, infrastructure, and community
  development

- General governmental activities

Each team had three objectives:

- Identify immediate opportunities for increasing
  efficiency and improving cost-effectiveness that
  could be realized by executive or administrative
  order.

- Suggest managerial, operating, and organizational
  improvements for both immediate and long-term
  consideration by the mayor and city council.

- Pinpoint specific areas where further in-depth analysis could be justified by potential short- or long-term benefits.

It soon became apparent that two major factors were dragging the city down: the lack of a systemic management approach and a dearth of trained and experienced managers.

The final report of the task force contained more than six hundred specific recommendations to improve the operations of city government. The task force study, if fully implemented, would result in an estimated one-time savings of $37 million and potential savings of $30 million annually.[1]

But then what?

Implementation

As I noted earlier, the personal commitment of the mayor or other city executive is a key element in the success of any P3 plan. One of the most important things that you can do is set a positive tone for your managers and foster a culture of professionalism through all levels of administration. Part of that professionalism is the discipline to follow through, to *implement* the plan developed.[2]

First, you should *set expectations* for implementation. In Cleveland, using the OITF's final report for guidance, each department head was required to write an implementation plan proposing middle- and long-term strategies for managing budgets and improving the delivery of services in their own departments. Because I had established good working relationships with department heads and commissioners, they understood that this was not to be a punitive action—though I also made it clear that progress would be the measure of their performance evaluations.

At first, the OITF leadership oversaw the plan, but in 1981, supervision of implementation progress passed from the OITF to my law director and chief of staff, Tom Wagner. He began tracking and reporting on the implementation progress in each department. By 1982, an astounding 94 percent of the task force's recommendations had already been implemented or were in process, at which time the OITF reported that its goals had been achieved and that its work was concluded.

As a newly elected official, you may be sticking your neck out and taking political risks by reaching out to businesses and other community groups to propose creating a P3 like the OITF. At the same time, the potential rewards in terms of productivity and more efficient delivery of public services are even greater. There are also significant intangible benefits, including establishing a culture of professionalism in city government and opening channels of communication between the public and private sectors. Indeed, many of the loaned executives from the Cleveland P3 stayed in touch with their city counterparts long after the official OITF had ended. This type of relationship that carries over even after the initial project is completed helps sustain the progress that you've achieved. More about that later.

three

The Audit

Even before I officially began my first term as mayor, I got some disturbing news: the City of Cleveland's books were not auditable. This was an immense problem, and one that further exposed the financial and administrative mess in which the city was mired. While there were many other things on my plate, including attracting top talent to the administration and creating a financial supervisory commission, I knew that one of the first priorities was to discern exactly what the city's true financial situation was. As the former auditor of Cuyahoga County, I also knew that we needed a high level of professional help to achieve that.

Even before the election, I had reached out to a number of Cleveland accounting firms with the help of Jim Delaney, who was then the managing partner of Deloitte.[1] He helped organize our first meeting and committed his firm to participating in a pro bono audit of the city's books. Why? Because it was in his and his firm's best interest, as well as that of the public. That audit would get our finances into a state fit enough for us to evaluate what needed to be done immediately to keep the city afloat.

The day after I took office, a volunteer group of accountants marshaled by the OITF began taking an inventory of Cleveland's financial situation. After eleven weeks, they established that the city was $110 million in debt, more than double the previous estimate. This volunteer group, led by executives from Ernst & Young, included representatives from seven of Cleveland's eight major accounting firms, as well as from the city's biggest corporations: Standard Oil, Eaton, TRW, and the Chessie System (later known as CSX). The value of this audit by such a highly experienced group of accountants was more than $350,000, something that the city could never have afforded. The credibility of those performing the audit ensured its wide acceptance by the financial community, including Wall Street, as an accurate depiction of Cleveland's financial condition.

Then it was time to find the right person for the post of finance director. In a city like Cleveland, the finance director is the equivalent of a chief financial officer in the private sector. The director's responsibilities include oversight of the city's accounting and financial reporting, as well as communications and coordination with external organizations, such as banks, auditors, rating agencies, and financial advisers.

Again, I turned to the private sector. A few days after the election, Jim Delaney agreed to chair the search committee to recruit a highly qualified finance director. That committee interviewed candidates from San Francisco, Philadelphia, San Antonio, and other cities. As a result, we met Bill Reidy, who then was with PricewaterhouseCoopers. We all found Bill impressive. He was a native Clevelander and well regarded by the business community. He soon became the consensus candidate.

Bill was quick to let me know that the city's financial house could be put back into order but that it would take a tremendous amount of work. That's why he and his team were so vital. "The city was in default of its loans payable to local banks—$14 million in debt," Bill told us. "The city had lost its investment grade credit rating—and then you had the state auditor declaring the city's records to be unauditable. . . . The city was using cash-basis financial reporting, which was an outdated and unacceptable practice. What all this meant was that the city's accounting practices were unreliable and needed to be replaced. Also, the staff of the city's finance office needed to be reorganized and strengthened, and a more qualified accounting staff had to be added."[2]

The OITF recommended that we increase the salaries of directors. There was some doubt as to whether the city council would approve that measure, but they did—at least in part because George Forbes, president of the council, was on the Financial Planning and

Supervision Commission (FPSC) appointed by the state to oversee Cleveland's finances during the fiscal emergency. I had made a point of forging a partnership with George when I became mayor, a relationship that helped smooth the path for further reforms in the difficult days ahead. More about that later.

The FPSC came into being after Harry Lehman, Democratic state representative from the Cleveland suburb of Beachwood, introduced Ohio HB 132 in late 1978 as a response to Cleveland's default. After some delay, it passed in 1979 by large majorities in both the House and the Senate. In addition to George and me, the commission consisted of five others: George Grabner, president of Lamson & Sessions; Jackie Presser, the well-known leader of Teamsters Union District No. 41; Mary Ellen Withrow, Ohio's state treasurer; William Shkurti, director of Ohio's Office of Budget and Management; and Robert Blyth, president of National City Bank. The audit firm of Deloitte acted as the commission's financial supervisor.

The commission was to disband only when three conditions were met. First, the city would have to plan and implement a financial accounting system within two years. Second, the objectives of the financial plan would have to be met, including a balanced budget and no deficits. Third, the fiscal conditions that caused the commission to be appointed under HB 132 in the first place would have to be resolved. In Cleveland's case, this was the default on its debt. The OITF also recommended a spending limit as a requirement to get Cleveland on firm financial ground.

The FPSC took a number of steps to create the environment to fulfill the three conditions. First, we approved the city's proposed financial bailout plan and set out its objectives. On October 8, 1980, eight banks agreed to purchase up to $36 million in twelve-year bonds, putting Cleveland back in the bond market with a rating from Moody's and Standard & Poor's that was better than that of many other cities. Then, on February 17, 1981, voters passed an increase in the city's income tax, by a remarkable 65,326 to 38,902 votes.

Of course, none of this could have happened without Bill Reidy and his team. During his two years as finance director, they

- reorganized the accounting department to function more effectively and hired additional, more qualified staff;

- implemented a new accounting system (FAMIS), which allowed the city to strengthen controls and improve its financial reporting;

- allowed a one-time $280,000 payment for the city to provide the data necessary for an audit of the records according to generally accepted accounting principles;

- engaged the firm of Ernst & Young as the city's independent auditors; and

- budgeted $200,000 per year to create the Division of Financial Reporting and Control.

The division established financial controls to prevent future fiscal problems and to enable the city to maintain accurate accounting records and issue a comprehensive annual financial report. Bill Reidy worked closely with the FPSC to help satisfy their oversight requirements. The city prepared a financial plan for fiscal years 1980, 1981, and 1982, as required by HB 132, and submitted it to the FPSC, which accepted and approved it.

We met with ratings agencies to demonstrate the improvement to the city's financial operations and financial strength. This resulted in the restoration of an investment-grade rating in July 1981. I'll never forget that date, because it occurred two days after we illuminated the Terminal Tower, which was the tallest building in Cleveland at the time and which had gone dark several years earlier, as a cost-saving move.

It was a symbol that Cleveland was back.

The icing on the cake came on Friday, June 26, 1987, when the last of the city's $110 million debt was paid off with a $1.1 million check. I made sure that Bill was there to see this celebration. While he was no longer the city's finance director, he continued to help us out as an unpaid consultant, and later, when I became governor, he helped me put together an operations improvement task force at the state level. It is worth noting that two members of Bill's team, Dan Neckel and Phil Allen, went on to serve as finance directors of the City of Cleveland. Bill's service is a perfect example of how powerful and critical a P3 can be. It was the key to my success as mayor of the City of Cleveland and later as governor of Ohio.

The big lessons from Cleveland's fiscal and financial recovery are these: *Don't ignore the problem* and hope that it will go away—and certainly don't try to hide it. If you are honest with the banks, regulators, and voters, they will be more likely to respect you and your proposals and thus more likely to hear you out. *Listen to the advice of experts* and take advantage of their knowledge. This is one of the most basic elements in a successful P3: if you are offered good counsel, take it, regardless of the source and even if you have to swallow some pride. Ultimately, you will have to make some tough decisions. *Remember always that you are in service to your city and your constituents* and that securing their future is your ultimate goal.

four

The Cleveland OITF and
Total Quality Management

I can look back now with satisfaction on what Cleveland's P3 was able to accomplish. At the same time, however, I can see where we might have done even more if we'd had access to certain organizational tools that are well known today but were still in their early days then. One of these is Total Quality Management (TQM), which I found tremendously useful in my terms as governor of the state and which would have been of great value in our work in Cleveland. Back then, we were discovering on our own many of the same pathways to organizational restructuring and re-form that today are part of the TQM model. Although I can apply its principles to the Cleveland OITF only in retrospect, TQM can be a valuable addition to your tool kit as you look ahead at the challenges facing your city.

TQM, in a nutshell, is a management philosophy of *alignment and integration* of functions across an organization—be it a small business, a large corporation, or a local or state government—to focus on serving the needs of customers or constituents. It relies on the concept of *continuous improvement*, by which the organization and its units constantly measure their performance and set new standards for efficiency and service. And finally, *employee input* is of great importance in the TQM process; after all, they're the experts on their own jobs.

The major challenge in getting the private sector to commit time and money to a P3—besides persuading business leaders that it would improve the quality of life in their community—is convincing them that an elected or appointed chief executive will actually implement their recommendations. I gave them my word and stuck to it. It seems simple, but the more that you keep your promises, the more trust you will build with your private-sector partners. Every business deal, every contract is based on trust that the other side will perform as promised. Corporate leaders understand this, and if you show them that you understand it too, you've taken the first and perhaps most important step toward a productive partnership.

I also made it clear from the beginning that I desired to involve, fully, the people who worked for the city. I was genuinely interested in their best ideas for improving the city's performance in terms of efficiency, cost reduction, and the quality and delivery of services. In my kickoff meeting with the task force participants, I told them, "I think you'll find city employees willing and eager to help. They have been ignored and passed over too often, and now they will have a real chance to offer their suggestions. It's an opportunity I'm sure they will be grateful for."

This idea first came to me when I was Cuyahoga County auditor, conducting the first-ever management audit of a county office. I noticed that many of the best ideas came from our own employees, most of whom had never been asked how their departments could work better and smarter. Later, when I went to the U.S. Senate, I saw that when federal agency employees were threatened by the privatization of their jobs and were given an opportunity to compete to keep them, they won 85 percent of the time. Why? Because often it was their first opportunity to make a case for how they could be more competitive.

But back to Cleveland.

Because our twenty-five city unions were familiar with the goals of the OITF, and seven of them even had contributed money to the effort, they cooperated with the task force and thus were able to influence the recommendations. When we decided that a tax increase was necessary, they agreed before the vote to limit their demand for a wage increase. I was fortunate in that my liaison to the unions was Jackie Presser, who was at that time the president of the local chapter of the Teamsters

International and vice chair of the Financial Planning and Supervision Commission.

As I previously noted, former mayor Dennis Kucinich had alienated the city council and particularly George Forbes, its long-standing president, who was a powerful and sometimes contentious figure in his own right. I knew that if I wanted the task force to succeed, I needed George's support. During the primary, he had opposed me. After the primary, however, he changed his mind and came around to support me, perhaps in part because of his relationship with the incumbent mayor, who he felt did not treat him with dignity and respect. I also knew George personally because his daughter Mildred and my son George were classmates in the Cleveland public schools. I immediately communicated to him my belief that the mayor's office and the city council had a symbiotic relationship and that only by working together could we move the city ahead.

The first thing I did was put George's name on all city stationery, symbolizing our partnership. When the Cleveland Advertising Club wanted to honor me, I insisted that they honor both of us. Needless to say, the council became supportive of the task force recommendations because they knew that we were partners—a "public-public partnership." The bottom line was that George and I were a team. I recall with pride what *USA Today* wrote about the two of us when we both retired: "Sunday is the last day in office for Mayor George Voinovich and City Council President George Forbes, who are generally credited with turning the nation's 22nd largest city from a laughingstock in the 1970s into a three-time All-America City winner during the 1980s. . . . Both men say the key to their success was working together."[1]

On the city's OITF, I gave Tom Wagner, my law director and chief of staff, the responsibility of monitoring implementation. Tom was a young partner at Calfee, Halter & Griswold, the law firm with which I was associated for two years after becoming county commissioner. I got to know Tom through the law office and at events sponsored by the Council of Smaller Enterprises, the small-business adjunct of our chamber of commerce. Tom was clearly concerned about Cleveland's plight and the negative impact that it was having on the economic future of the region.

Tom later told me that he was motivated to join my administration for a number of reasons, including his sense of community service. Also, he said, "Cleveland was rapidly deteriorating and that was not conducive to either raising a family or growing a law practice in Cleveland. I knew that [Mayor Voinovich] had the highest ethical standards and a reputation for honestly addressing and solving problems."[2] Tom, like Bill Reidy, my finance director, is an example of a person from the private sector who came into government, made enormous contributions, and then returned better equipped for success in his or her respective organization. Ultimately, I asked Tom to take on the responsibilities of implementing the task force recommendations. He was uniquely qualified because, as chief administrative officer, he focused on having departments communicate with each other to solve problems and find necessary resources.

Initially, some task force members were frustrated because some of the recommendations were not implemented immediately. Tom, who had great interpersonal skills, had to explain that getting things done in the public sector can be more difficult than in the private sector. He took the time to review with the task force members the legal requirements that had to be met to make the various recommended changes, such as an amendment to the city charter or action by the city council.

Tom met with each department head to determine all the issues and answer their questions about the implementation of recommendations, the additional resources required, and the timeline for each—and he made sure there was constant follow-up. His close monitoring and strong relationships with city employees helped fuel our success, as did frequent meetings between task force groups and city directors, on both a formal and an informal basis.

Each city director was charged with producing a weekly report to show progress in implementation of the plan in his or her department. As I mentioned, I made it clear that progress toward departmental goals would be a crucial component of their performance evaluations—never as a threat, but as a way of setting clear expectations. It's also important to recognize success. For example, each month, I had Tom present an Eagle Award to the director making the most progress. It was fun, and it conveyed our appreciation for their hard work.

That's how we did it in Cleveland. We achieved our goal of putting the city back on an even keel, and in the process, we all learned a lot about the power of P3s to bring about change. And that knowledge and experience stood me in good stead for the next challenge.

The State Operations Improvement Task Force and TQM

By the time that I ran for governor in 1990, I knew better than anyone how critical the OITF had been to Cleveland's renewal. So, early on in my campaign, I committed to conducting an OITF on the state level.

I was fortunate that Bob Van Auken, a retired president of Union Commerce Bank who had worked with me when I was mayor, volunteered to help my campaign. Because I faced no primary opposition and had good prospects for the general election, Bob could devote time to recruiting volunteers for the planned state OITF. He also reviewed applications for positions in my cabinet. The fact that I did not seek reelection as mayor in 1989 and did nothing but campaign in 1990 also helped in putting the team together; it allowed me to meet personally with many of the job candidates.

Once I was elected, I asked Bob to manage the state-level task force. When we announced the initiative to state employees, two major concerns arose.

First, how many jobs were going to be cut? And second, would we come up with a lot of pie-in-the-sky ideas that would never be implemented? Potential job losses were a concern, but people also knew that in Cleveland very few jobs had been lost, and that mitigated their fear somewhat.

In the state-level OITF, more than three hundred people donated upward of 150,000 hours. They made nearly 1,600 recommendations of ways to save money, absorb budget cuts without sacrificing quality, and eliminate duplication and waste. If the state had paid for their time and support services, the tab would have run to $14 million.

The volunteers served in one of five groups:

1. The leadership panel, consisting of forty Ohio business and institutional leaders, supplied oversight and core support. Leadership panelists came from Ohio's largest corporations and institutions, including Banc One, Dayton Power & Light, Goodyear, Nationwide Insurance, and the Ohio State University.

2. The project managers were representatives of two public accounting firms, Deloitte and Coopers & Lybrand. Their task was to advise teams on review methods and to ensure the validity of results.

3. The agency group leaders were seven executives from OITF sponsoring companies, each of whom oversaw six to eight specialized teams that investigated related

functions, a sort of middle management. For example, one team might review all the state's activities related to health inspections.

4. The task force leaders were thirty-five executives who supervised daily activities of task force members. They were responsible for reporting the results.

5. The task force members were nearly two hundred volunteers from sponsoring companies who collected and analyzed information in every state agency. This involved a review of facts, figures, recommendations, and opinions from state employees, from chairs of corresponding legislative committees, and from employees of each agency. These reports also included comments from people who wrote or phoned in ideas.

Most of the agency reviews were conducted between March and September 1991, though some weren't finished until 1993. The work of the state OITF did not end with the review process, however. Key volunteers returned to their posts periodically to monitor progress on recommendations. At six-month intervals, they confirmed which recommendations had been implemented, which efforts still needed to be corrected, and which were on track.

Eleven of the recommendations were considered "global issues" that extended beyond the boundaries of any one department. The first of those was fundamental to implementing the rest of the task force recommendations. It urged us to focus on our "customers," both internal and external; to facilitate team building, employee contribution and responsibility, risk taking, and innovation; to analyze our systems and procedures to uncover inefficiencies and ways to ameliorate them; and to pursue the goal of continuous improvement. In other words, the OITF urged the State of Ohio to adopt the concept of TQM.

I was somewhat familiar with the principles of TQM, which came from the work of famed management consultant W. Edwards Deming. His philosophy was embraced first in Japan and then later in the United States. To my knowledge, at that time, it had not yet been adopted by any state government.

But I also wondered whether we had exhausted our help from the private sector. If we had, how would we get this done?

Fortunately, just then, I got a visit from representatives from Xerox, who informed me that the company wanted to assist us with the state OITF. I explained that the task force had completed its work but that we might be able to use their help in following up on recommendations. When they told me how they had implemented TQM under the chairmanship of David Kearns, I asked if they would be willing to help me introduce and adapt it for the State of Ohio. They said yes. I knew that if we could make TQM part of state government, it would empower our employees to maximize their own talent and grow in their jobs. I also believed that it would reduce the cost of government, make us more efficient and effective, and improve the quality of the services that we provided to Ohio residents.

Jack Kindell, a top executive thoroughly familiar with TQM, came to work with us, adapting training materials based on the Xerox model for use by state employees and senior managers. We selected seven agencies as pilots to implement TQM and then adopted a purpose statement that read, "The purpose of Quality Services through Partnership (QStP) is to transform Ohio government into an organization in which all employees work together to continuously improve how work is done. This transformation is a partnership between management and unions representing state employees. It is accomplished by learning and practicing in collaboration the best known principles, problem-solving processes, and tools used to make organizations effective and efficient. The goal is for state government's customers, the citizens of Ohio, to know they are getting value for their tax dollars."[3]

Xerox's commitment to help introduce TQM to Ohio state government was nothing less than awesome. We calculated the value of Jack's time and of the loaned executives and the materials provided by the company at $3 million. We also hired someone to assist Jack and to provide other administrative and clerical help.

I should note, however, that we didn't call it TQM. We decided to change the name to Quality Services through Partnership (QStP), because it was the term preferred by one of our other major partners, the unions. In my opinion, the initiative succeeded in large part because of the partnerships we established with union leaders, particularly with Paul Goldberg, executive director of the Ohio Civil Service Employees Association, and the presidents of the state's other four major labor unions: the Fraternal Order of Police, United Food and Commercial Workers, Ohio Education Association, and Ohio Health Care Employees.

Goldberg once said that one reason why QStP is important is that it gives employees a powerful voice: "In the past, government workers have been caught between a stifling bureaucracy and a public that expects good, efficient services. Workers were becoming dangerously alienated, yet they held the key to redesigning government. The person doing the job knows best how to improve it, but unfortunately, no one was listening to them."[4] QStP, for the first time, gave state workers a way to speak out and to apply their ideas.

It was a partnership unheard of in the history of labor and management in U.S. state government. Looking back, I believe that adopting QStP was the most significant initiative that I undertook as governor. Without it, we would not have been able to implement fully the recommendations of the state OITF. QStP resulted in the most significant improvement in state government in anyone's memory.

I spent more time on QStP than on any other initiative that I undertook as governor because I understood that my personal involvement, as in Cleveland, would be key to its success. It gave me great satisfaction that when I left the governor's office, all twenty-eight state agencies were participating in the program. In total, some 250 union and management trainers were provided, and more than fifty thousand of our employees participated in training. It was and still is the best way that I know to give state and city governments the tools necessary to recruit, retain, reward, and manage their most important asset: their people.

This journey toward greater quality and efficiency began in 1991, and although it lost some momentum after I left state government for the U.S. Senate, its effects continue to this day. In 2013, Governor John Kasich and the state legislature even instituted a program that provides scholarships to local government employees to learn TQM, or, as it is called today, Lean Six Sigma.

As you've read this brief account of the state-level OITF and considered its similarities to and differences from the strategies used in the Cleveland turnaround, I hope that you've also contemplated its applicability to your situation in your own city. Could a Lean Six Sigma program help you or your city managers and employees? Chances are good that at least one private-sector company in your partnership has experience with the program and could provide valuable insight into how it could improve govern-ment services. Perhaps OITF partners would even fi-nance training for a trial group of city departments or agencies. In any case and by any name—TQM, QStP, or Lean Six Sigma—it worked for Cleveland and the State of Ohio, and it could work for you.

five

The Mayor's Operation
Volunteer Effort and How to
Sustain Your Gains

The Cleveland OITF proved to be an effective means for achieving the goals set forth in its planning documents. A first partnership, if it is successful, can build synergy between the public and private sectors and make a community receptive to establishing other partnerships to tackle other challenges.

There's another and perhaps greater benefit, too: participation can inspire leaders in the private sector to contribute to the public good not just through partnerships but also through philanthropy and other means that provide benefits across the community.

This chapter draws on contributions and perspectives by Annie Lewis Garda and Morton Mandel.

A stellar example is Morton Mandel, who was at that time the CEO of Premier Industrial.

"What motivated me was that I cared about Cleveland," Mort told me. "I know that is going to sound corny, but there are people who do things to create a better quality of life. . . . I thought there was a chance I could help Cleveland become a better place to live, work and raise a family."[1] Mort was part of the inner circle that put the OITF together, raised the money for it, and provided loaned executives, including his company's chief of purchasing.

Mort is a liberal Democrat who once was very active on the Democratic National Committee, but he described our relationship as apolitical, "not Republican or Democrat." We quickly became friends, despite our political differences, and I can't recall a time when we met over the years that we did not conspire to create yet another new partnership that would benefit the city, state, or country. I believe that his involvement with the Cleveland OITF helped expand his already strong civic consciousness and contributed to his lifetime of deeds on behalf of the community. Mort's involvement, leadership, and philanthropy in Cleveland and in the Jewish community have become legendary.

We worked together to create Cleanland Ohio (now the LAND Studio), the Mid Town Corridor (now MidTown Cleveland), and Cleveland Tomorrow. In 1984, he founded the Mandel Center for Nonprofit Organizations at Case Western Reserve University and, more recently, the Jack, Joseph and Morton Mandel

Humanities Center at Cleveland State University. He has also given the largest-ever donation to Cuyahoga Community College: a $10 million gift to construct a center focused on creating civically responsible citizens who will lead northeast Ohio toward a stronger economic and social future.

After we had begun implementing the recommendations of the OITF, Mort called me and said that he wanted to get together to discuss an idea. He suggested that since the OITF was such a success, we should keep it going, and he offered to pick up the tab to pay an individual to work at city hall to coordinate a new entity called the Mayor's Operation Volunteer Effort (MOVE).

The program had two main components.

The first, called the Loaned Executive Committee, was chaired by Jack Dwyer of Oglebay Norton and composed of executives recruited at the request of city administrators to solve specific problems. This loaned executive program differed from the model used in the original OITF in that the executives worked directly with and reported to city administrators during their time at city hall. Most often, they provided part-time rather than full-time service, as the OITF execs had done.

The second committee oversaw a citizen volunteer group made up of people who stepped forward and wanted to donate their time and talent to the city's cause. This committee was chaired by Jim Delaney of Deloitte.

When Annie Lewis Garda came on board as coordinator of MOVE, the last piece was in place. She was already an active volunteer, serving on the boards of several nonprofit organizations. She was the perfect person for the job.

At first, Cleveland corporations and foundations covered all expenses for Project MOVE. And even after the city took on the day-to-day operating costs, our private-sector partners—most notably Premier Industrial's foundation—continued to fund our annual volunteer recognition event and other special projects.

Loaned Executive Program

On the loaned executive side of the program, Annie Lewis Garda worked with city managers to develop their requests, which she then took to the Loaned Executive Committee. Committee members either volunteered the services of executives from their respective companies or recruited an executive from another company. After introducing the executive to the requesting city administrator, Annie tracked progress on the project and provided regular updates to the committee.

In the first year alone, loaned executives and their public-sector counterparts completed no fewer than twenty-five projects. For example, an executive from Stouffer's worked for six months with the city's data center to develop procedures for security, disaster protection, and user communication. In another case, graduate students from the Weatherhead School of Business at Case Western Reserve University worked with water pollution control to develop a computerized system for handling complaints. Two executives from Dalton-Dalton-Newport (now AECOM) developed an information management system for the City Planning Commission, and Oglebay Norton sent an executive to work on new procedures to reduce police overtime.

Volunteer Program

There were two main ways by which citizen volunteers came to city hall. In the first, a city employee filled out a volunteer request form to be sent to one or more volunteer recruitment and placement agencies, such as the Community Information/Volunteer Action Center, the Retired Senior Volunteer Program, the Greater Cleveland Connection, and the Cleveland Senior Council. In other cases, the organizations themselves forwarded to the project coordinator the names of potential volunteers whose skills might match some of the city's needs.

For example, a volunteer certified public accountant wrote procedure manuals for several city departments. In another case, volunteers helped organize a folk-art exhibition sponsored by the Department of Aging. A retired artist illustrated the annual report of the Landmarks Commission. And there was always a cadre of volunteers who gave tours of city hall.

Hundreds of volunteers already were working in the city's recreation centers, so Project MOVE reached out to support them. Over brown-bag lunches in the mayor's office, supervisors in the various service programs discussed common problems in the recruitment and management of volunteers. The solution: a handbook for supervisors and a handbook for volunteers.

People were donating thousands of hours of time and labor to their city, so it was only fitting that the city recognize those efforts. Thus began our annual volunteer recognition event, jointly hosted by my office and the city council, to express our appreciation of the volunteers and all of their hard work. Dianne Scaravilli, president of the Cleveland Junior League, came up with the idea of establishing a mayor's award to recognize the efforts of the community's most outstanding volunteers. The Community Information/Volunteer Action Center, with financial support from American Greetings, organized the event, taking nominations, selecting judges, and hosting a reception at city hall to honor all semifinalists.

The Public Relations Advisory Board

The Public Relations Advisory Board came about when members of the Volunteer Committee realized that many city departments were requesting assistance in that area. The board, chaired by David Leahy, a former regional manager of Sears, Roebuck, met monthly with my office's press secretary to review requests from city directors. Projects included creating a marketing plan for Cleveland Public Power, helping develop a brochure for the Economic Development Department, updating old slide presentations for the Health

Department, and promoting the All-America City celebration. The board also looked for private sources of funding to help take projects from the drawing board to reality.

For my part, I set a positive tone and encouraged full cooperation by city workers with our private-sector partners in pursuit of our common goals: continuous improvement of city services and a better quality of life for all of its citizens. Many of those who participated, whether loaned executives or civic volunteers, later said that they had found the work rewarding on a personal or professional level.

Legacy of the State QStP

As noted in the previous chapter, we succeeded in replicating the Cleveland OITF at the state level when I became governor. Ohio's major corporations and other organizations, such as the Ohio Manufacturers Association and the Ohio Chamber of Commerce, realized that the model worked and that there was a symbiotic relationship with the state. I decided, and the corporate leaders agreed, that we needed a state organization of CEOs modeled after Cleveland Tomorrow. The result was the Ohio Business Roundtable (BRT).

Bob Van Auken, manager of the QStP, joined a cadre of volunteer CEOs to lay the foundations of the BRT. Among them were Tim Timken of the Timken Company, Tim Smucker of Smucker's, Western & Southern's John Barrett, Mead's Burnell Roberts, and most notably, BF Goodrich's John Ong (who at the time also chaired the National Business Roundtable). These five CEOs believed that business leaders should have an active and effective role in the formulation and evaluation of public policy. With a single, unified voice representing the state's principal business leaders, the five charter members recruited fifty of their peers who also recognized the vision and leadership that such a body could provide to state policy makers. And so the BRT was born, and for the past twenty-five years, it has continued to foster a collaborative and constructive bond between Ohio's private- and public-sector leaders.

With support from the worldwide consulting firm McKinsey, the BRT tackled what I once characterized as "Ohio's silent killer of jobs," our beleaguered workers' compensation system, and helped transform it into a distinctive public asset. Next up was a twenty-year marathon to reform Ohio's K–12 education system through higher standards, rigorous assessments, and accountability for results. Over time, school choice, STEM education, and the bookend issues of early childhood education and college completion were added to the agenda.

The Third Frontier, which today is Ohio's preeminent technology commercialization platform, would not exist but for the BRT's early and sustained advocacy. The BRT also incubated Governor John Kasich's signature (privatized) economic development program, JobsOhio. This was also true for its predecessor, the

Ohio Business Development Coalition, under Governors Bob Taft and Ted Strickland. Initiatives in childhood obesity, patient safety, electronic records, consumer value consciousness, Medicaid, and long-term care cost control also were outgrowths of this work. And, finally, on traditional business climate issues, the BRT worked vigorously on civil justice and tort reform and helped enact the state's most comprehensive tax policy reforms.

It's fair to say that the nonpartisan Ohio BRT remained focused on its own North Star: nurturing Ohio as a special place for people to live, learn, and pursue their dreams.

six

The Pivotal Role of Foundations

The Cleveland OITF would not have become such a great success had the Cleveland and Gund Foundations not gotten involved in the financing, oversight, and monitoring of the implementation of the OITF recommendations.

First, some history. The Cleveland Foundation, established in 1914, was the first community foundation in the country. The George Gund Foundation was set up as a private nonprofit institution in 1952 by George Gund, the president and CEO of Cleveland Trust, which at one time was the eighteenth-largest bank in the United States.

This chapter draws on correspondence and perspectives from David T. Abbott, executive director of the George Gund Foundation, and Robert B. Jaquay, associate director.

Many communities have foundations, though they may not be as old or as large as Cleveland's. Sometimes the leadership of those foundations thinks that it would be inappropriate for their organizations to get involved with the challenges confronting their local and state governments. In some ways, this is understandable, because foundations generally don't want to get caught up in the political fray. This attitude can hold foundations back, however, when they could play an active role in shaping the future of their home cities.

The history of the Cleveland Foundation is instructive in terms of the evolution that it underwent, one that took it to a place where it became intimately involved with the governance of the city. I believe that this change occurred because of the enlightened leadership of the Cleveland Foundation's presidents over the years and the participation of engaged citizens on their allocation committees.

In a paper titled "The Foundation and Municipal Governance: Helping the City Do Its Work," the Cleveland Foundation describes its evolution from an entity that simply gathered a great deal of data to one that actively participated in the Cleveland turnaround. In its early years and through the 1960s, the foundation focused on promoting social change through surveys, an approach informed by the philosophy that "to give the population the exact facts would lead to public remedy."[1] But slowly it became clear to the leaders of the foundation that this passive approach was no longer sufficient. So they waded, reluctantly at first, into the public sphere. By then, economic and social conditions in Cleveland had begun to deteriorate, starting in the 1970s and continuing into the early 1980s. In 1978, in fact, a team of six researchers, backed by the Cleveland Foundation and contracted through the Brookings Institution, concluded that the city was "virtually a ward of the federal government."[2] It was time for action, not just information gathering.

The foundation encouraged a leading urban researcher, George E. Peterson of the Urban Institute in Washington, DC, to include Cleveland in an upcoming Housing and Urban Development–funded study of the infrastructure of a number of America's cities. City leaders needed to know just what kind of physical shape Cleveland was in. To no one's surprise, Peterson's study found that almost every aspect of Cleveland's infrastructure was in disrepair. He estimated that it would take $2 billion to pay for the necessary repairs and reconstruction. Later, the Cleveland Foundation contributed another $100,000 for a study to develop a realistic strategy to finance the rehabilitation of the city's roads, bridges, water systems, and sewers.[3]

By this time, the Cleveland Foundation had formulated a new goal for aiding the city. It would provide the start-up money and technical experts who would give city officials the tools they needed. The foundation agreed to contribute $150,000 toward establishing the OITF on two conditions: first, that some of that money be used to implement the task force's recommendations, and second, that those funds would be matched by other donations. By the time that the OITF made its recommendations, the foundation was already positioned to assist with their implementation.

It did so by funding advanced management training in public health, higher education, and government. Foundation grants paid for short courses on management, taught at Case Western Reserve and Harvard Universities, which several high-level Cleveland officials completed. They paid for other classes, too, including a management course specifically designed for senior city officials. The city received another grant for general personnel training; professional development had been woefully neglected for many years, and it showed.

Responding to another recommendation from the OITF, the foundation funded a new human resources management system that captured details on job classifications, compensation, and performance appraisal. The city had never had such a system, and it was sorely needed. These funds were separate from and in addition to the monies provided for the OITF. The lesson here? Always ask.

The Cleveland Foundation also was instrumental in the city's passing a recommended 0.5 percent income tax increase. How did they do that? First, by doing some research. The foundation paid for a study that found that Cleveland had a lower tax liability than most comparably sized cities. This finding was persuasive enough to convince voters to approve the tax increase, even though they had refused—twice—to do so in the recent past. The increase raised a much-needed $35 million.

Taking a close look at the city's safety department, the foundation encouraged the development of a Police Stress Unit consisting of a few police officers and a psychologist. The unit was designed to assist police officers in alleviating some of the stress that they dealt with on the job each day. Such stress, unchecked, was leading to alcohol abuse and other destructive behaviors on the part of police officers. The foundation also backed the creation of an Integrated Safety System designed to streamline and computerize police calls and other information sharing. This new system decreased both paperwork and duplication in the department and resulted in a more responsive police force. One local newspaper noted that this initiative was equivalent to redirecting the work of fifty-seven full-time police officers away from desk duty and back to patrolling the streets and assisting residents.

The foundation also commissioned the RAND Corporation to complete a major economic analysis of the region to uncover why some industries in northeast Ohio were struggling while others were thriving. Another grant paid for a computer-based Land Information System that provided clear information on the ownership and availability of parcels of land throughout the city so that this real estate could be used for development.

Essentially, the Cleveland Foundation's role, before and after the OITF, was a reinterpretation and extension of its old mission: to provide the kind of intelligence needed for action. By illuminating problems and then providing a jumpstart for solutions, the foundation acted as a steward for the public and provided a lubricant to smooth government functioning.

When criticized or threatened, government agencies and officeholders can become territorial and defensive; the role of the foundation as an outside and neutral party was crucial to overcoming this kind of resistance. The foundation was able to view Cleveland government as a whole, identify problems where its expertise could prove useful, make specific recommendations, and sometimes provide the seed money required for action.

On many occasions when I thought that something needed to be done, I simply picked up the phone and called Homer Wadsworth, then the president of the Cleveland Foundation. In most instances, I would be asking for something that the city could not afford or for help with a project that I knew the city council was unlikely to approve. Homer usually would find a way to help us achieve what we needed to do.

For example, for almost fifty years, Cleveland had debated what to do with its lakefront. If not for the Cleveland Foundation's financing of a study to determine its best use, today there might be no Great Lakes Science Center or Rock and Roll Hall of Fame. Both are located at North Coast Harbor, which was built after a recommendation resulting from the study.

Another issue that I vividly recall arose when the owner of the Bulkley Building on Euclid Avenue in

Playhouse Square announced his plans to tear it down. He was unfazed by the fact that it housed two historic theaters, the State and the Palace, which the Playhouse Square Foundation wanted to restore. The Cleveland Foundation stepped in with an unprecedented investment of $3.9 million to purchase the building and save the theaters. If it had not done so, there would be no Playhouse Square as we know it today. It was and remains the largest theater restoration project in United States. In its entertainment capacity, it is second in size only to Lincoln Center in New York, and it brings to downtown Cleveland more than a million patrons each year.

None of this would have happened without the Cleveland Foundation's intercession.

But the George Gund Foundation was just as crucial to the Cleveland turnaround. The foundation not only contributed to funding the OITF but also helped finance studies on a broad range of topics, from infrastructure to enterprise zones and cable television franchise agreements. It also underwrote a variety of training and professional development opportunities for city personnel. The foundation played a key role in funding major development projects such as Lexington Village in the Hough neighborhood and the Great Lakes Science Center and the Rock and Roll Hall of Fame, without which our downtown lakefront would not be the gem it is today. In its work, the Gund Foundation has always emphasized the need to collaborate, and this willingness to work together toward common goals made it an invaluable partner in the OITF and long after.

David T. Abbott, the executive director of the Gund Foundation, is among the most knowledgeable people I've ever met on the subject of P3s. A former reporter and county administrator, he brings a unique set of skills and a fresh perspective on how city governments and the private sector can work together and how foundations can help them create effective urban programs.

David has written that the first step toward establishing a successful partnership is simply *recognizing that one is needed*: "Too often, individuals and organizations, driven by ego and a desire to be perceived as a leader, think they can make meaningful change on their own. That certainly can happen with simple problems, but progress in the civic environment is almost always a complex endeavor. Inevitably, there is no individual, organization or even sector with all of the necessary resources and ability. Collaboration is required."[4]

David's point is well illustrated by the example of the comprehensive planning project that came to be known as Civic Vision.[5] Revision of the city's master plan was among the more than six hundred recommendations of the OITF final report, but when it came to the implementation stage, the Cleveland and Gund Foundations urged city officials to go beyond a "planner's exercise" to one that also endeavored to develop a broad-based civic constituency for the community's future. Extensive consultation between city officials and neighborhood residents, business and banking leaders, ministers, ethnic group leaders, the staff of community development corporations and social service organizations, and many other constituencies led not only to updated zoning maps and development objectives but also to a shared sense of accomplishment. Civic Vision resulted in new and enduring working relationships and an increased appreciation of the need to continually expand civic networks. Lessons in collaboration from Civic Vision remain as valuable today as they were in the early 1980s.

You also have to understand that *every issue is different*. The partners needed to tackle one problem may not be the same ones required to solve another; the number, nature, and identity of the collaborators can and should vary. As David has noted, "Who initiates a partnership is less important than who is invited to the table. Sometimes a public executive such as a mayor or county official is well-positioned to bring people together. Sometimes a business organization or a nonprofit can effectively fill that role. Even a private citizen can do it." And, as he and I well know, it means finding people willing share the credit—or who simply don't care, as long as the work gets done.

The *timing* has to be right, too. It's not a partnership unless all participants have a meaningful voice in setting goals or developing strategies. Calling in people or organizations after the fact can make them far less willing to commit support. And why would they want to? If they feel that they have been invited only to foot the bill or to lend their prestige to a project without participating in its planning and execution, their motivation will plummet. Furthermore, you may miss out on good ideas or advice that those other potential partners could bring to the table.

Just as important as the goals, the participants, and the timing of an initiative is the *form or structure* that the partnership should take. Again, it depends on the problem being solved. And here, David has given more good advice: "Sometimes a problem requires a legal structure, such as a nonprofit corporation. In other instances, an informal or ad hoc group is the best response. This response, like the roster of participants, depends on the issue. Form should follow function."

Last, a word on the *limitations and potential pitfalls* of working with foundations. They can be good partners because of the resources at their disposal, but they also can have significant limitations on their own scope of action, which in turn may impose limitations on yours.

Foundations are creatures of their charters. Some are structured as nonprofit organizations. Others have been established as trusts. Some of them are run or advised by their major donor or donors, and some are established through testamentary bequests. In any case, the incorporators or founders get to set the terms under which the foundation will operate. There may be a cap on the dollar amounts of individual grants, for example, or constraints on the uses to which grant monies may be put. A foundation established to support the performing arts cannot fund a public utility infrastructure project, no matter how sympathetic the directors or trustees might be.

On the other hand, because they are accountable only to their boards, foundations enjoy certain advantages. They are free from the pressure of seeking reelection, and they don't have to meet the market's quarterly profit expectations.

Foundations can be very effective collaborators, and I've offered many examples here of successful projects from the Cleveland P3 in which they played key roles. Consider partnering with foundations in much the same way you would with a business, a union, or an association. Ask yourself (1) whether the issue or problem at hand is something that a foundation partner could help with—are they the right "person" for the right job?—and (2) how the foundation would fit within the organizational structure. If you decide that a foundation would be a good match for some aspect of the project, be sure to contact its representatives early in the planning process. But even before that, do your homework and carefully research the types of grants that the foundation was set up to make. Last, be sure to ask your other partners whether they have any contacts or relationships with people at the foundation. Individuals who sit on corporate or nonprofit boards may also serve on the board of directors or be trustees of private or community foundations.

Foundations were a big part of the Cleveland turnaround, and they may be part of your solution as well.

afterword

Thirty-Five Years Later

A Planner's Perspective

Hunter Morrison

I had the privilege of working with George Voinovich for his entire ten-year term as mayor of Cleveland. With the passage of time, I have had the opportunity to see the long-term benefits that resulted from the public-private partnerships he built during his administration.

Looking back, these partnerships seem obvious, even easy. At the time, they were neither.

In the early 1980s, civic collaboration was a foreign concept for Cleveland, a declining industrial city with an entrenched social order scarred by deep divisions of race, class, and ethnicity. Conflict—not collaboration—had defined social relationships and political behavior in Cleveland for well over a century. Asking historical combatants to turn their swords into plowshares was, to many at the time, a fool's errand— one destined to fail.

But that's exactly what Mayor Voinovich asked of his fellow Clevelanders.

Confronted by the stark reality of a bankrupt city crippled by political intrigue and class conflict, he charted a different course for his beloved hometown. He campaigned in the fall of 1979 on the slogan "Together We Can Do It." Over the next decade, he put that slogan to work in countless ways, big and small. Today, almost four decades after that fateful November election, Cleveland is a far different place than it would have been had it not changed course, learned how to build robust public-private partnerships, and created the civic capital that today enables it to compete at both national and global levels for talent and investment.

Simply put, together we *did* it.

More important, together we created new civic platforms, nonprofit organizations, academic programs, and professional networks that, two generations later, continue to support Cleveland's ongoing transformation.

I came into city government in the autumn of 1980, having worked for several years for the Hough Area Development Corporation, a community development corporation established in the aftermath of the 1967 Hough riots. I first met George Voinovich in the fall of 1979, when he was campaigning at Crawford Estates, a small subdivision of single-family houses that the corporation had developed and was successfully marketing. These were the first new for-sale houses built in the neighborhood in decades and one of the few hopeful stories to come out of Cleveland in the months following the city's default.

A year later, he asked me to join his administration and rebuild the City Planning Commission. I was in my early thirties at the time—but so were most of my fellow directors. We were young, energetic, inexperienced, and incredibly dedicated as a group to setting the city on the right course. The city government I joined was broke, demoralized, and dysfunctional. Warring political factions, entrenched bureaucratic practices, and obsolete city ordinances closed the door on the new thinking that the city needed if it was to move forward.

The Operations Improvement Task Force—and Mayor Voinovich's steadfast determination to see it implemented—became our North Star as we worked together to move our respective departments and divisions in new directions. The public-private partnership that was created to convene the Operations Improvement Task Force and oversee the implementation of its recommendations became a template for doing business differently in Cleveland.

Learning from this initial high-level partnership, the City Planning Commission went on to partner with neighborhood activists and the Cleveland chapter of the American Institute of Architects to prepare design and development plans to guide neighborhood reinvestment initiatives. For almost a decade, the commission partnered with the Kent State University College of Architecture and Environmental Design and local stakeholders to prepare detailed urban design studies for downtown Cleveland neighborhoods.

Throughout the process, we educated ourselves and our community counterparts in the art of successful collaboration. We developed a nuanced ability to work together and learned to leverage each other's strengths to prepare and implement complex community plans— plans that changed the face of downtown Cleveland and many of its neighborhoods. Our success with this small initial experiment in collaboration altered expectations, set new patterns of civic behavior, and built momentum to take on even more ambitious challenges.

After several years of working together to develop plans for individual neighborhoods and downtown districts, a broad community consensus emerged to support a more ambitious effort to update the city's official general plan. The last time the city had undertaken a downtown plan was in 1959, a decade before the spread of suburban shopping malls forever changed the face of the region's retail patterns. The citywide plan was even more outdated: completed in 1949, it reflected postwar optimism but failed to anticipate the dramatic impact that mass outmigration of people and jobs to adjacent suburbs would have on the city's population and economic base.

Clearly the city needed a new general plan that reflected both the economic realities that the city faced and the aspirations that its citizens had for their common future. The initiative to develop a new general plan came to be known as Civic Vision 2000. It consisted of four discrete but interconnected initiatives:

- A new citywide plan that replaced the 1949 plan and updated the city's land use, transportation, and development policies

- A new downtown plan that replaced the 1959 plan and addressed detailed urban design issues in downtown's emerging development districts

- Zoning recommendations that were used to update the city's obsolete zoning and mapping procedures and streamline the zoning review process

- A new citywide capital improvement plan that was used to align the city's annual capital budget with the recommendations made in the Civic Vision plans

A robust public-private partnership was at the heart of Civic Vision 2000. The public-sector team was led by the mayor and included representatives from county and state government. The private-sector team was led by Cleveland Tomorrow and included representatives of the city's business and philanthropic leadership. Together they raised more than $3 million in cash and in-kind services to hire the staff and consultants needed to undertake such a bold effort.

As they developed the new plans, the Civic Vision partners involved thousands of people from both the city and the surrounding suburbs in evening meetings, design charrettes, work sessions, and public hearings.

Civic Vision 2000 was completed in 1989 at the end of Mayor Voinovich's administration and fully adopted two years later. The downtown and citywide plans received national awards for excellence from the American Planning Association in 1992. In the decades that followed, Mayor Voinovich's three successors have carried out the Civic Vision plans and periodically updated them to ensure that the city's vision for its future would continue to be both clear and contemporary.

Mayor Voinovich's pioneering work of building collaboration through the use of public-private partnerships enabled a cash-strapped administration to "do more with less" by leveraging the goodwill, generosity, and abundant human capital assets of its corporations and philanthropies. We aligned, linked, and leveraged these resources to focus them on the major challenges Cleveland faced.

Over time, these successful public-private partnerships created a new collective mind-set. They changed the way Clevelanders worked together to address new and emerging challenges. Collaboration has replaced confrontation as the default response to an urgent civic issue—be it saving the Cleveland Browns football franchise, reorganizing the Cleveland Public Schools, or reforming police-community relations.

What lessons have we learned?

At the risk of oversimplifying a rich and nuanced story, let me suggest that there are seven broad lessons to take away from the city's experience with public-private partnerships:

1. *Respect and learn from each other.* Civic collaboration is a learned skill. Each participant has unique skills and insights to bring to the discussion. Mutual respect—and the behavior that promotes it—is critical to the success of a partnership.

2. *Link and leverage your community's assets.* Every community has a rich array of civic assets on which to build a more prosperous future. Use civic partnerships to identify, repurpose, and connect these assets in new ways to meet the needs of today and tomorrow.

3. *Focus on your shared future.* Public-private partnerships enable a community to set aside past practices and animosities and focus on what the partners can do together to build a future that is beneficial to all concerned. Through collaborations, partners learn to pursue their individual interests by contributing to the common good.

4. *Make a plan—then work the plan.* Public-private partnerships encourage mutual accountability and managed risks and increase the odds that your plan will be carried out. A culture of trust emerges when partners move ideas into action by taking countless small steps together. The lasting success

of the Operations Improvement Task Force came from carrying out the recommendations, not just making them.

5. *Do the doable—then do it again.* Successful partnerships learn to do by doing. Seemingly small achievements in the early days of a partnership teach the partners to work together and give them the confidence to tackle bigger challenges as time goes on. As trust builds, the partners develop the capacity to take on increasingly complex and sophisticated challenges.

6. *Celebrate your successes.* Declare victory as you accomplish each milestone in your plan. Over time, you will replace cynical expectations of failure with realistic expectations of success and build a record of civic accomplishment that attracts others to your community. You will create a new narrative—creative people doing interesting and important things together—that attracts others to your community.

7. *Strengthen your bench.* The formation of successful communities takes place over years, decades, and generations. Pass your hard-learned lessons on to the next generations by devoting the time and resources needed to create institutions, educational programs, civic networks, and community traditions. These will ensure that those who follow can build on your successes.

George Voinovich believed that the people expect their mayors and governors to provide trusted, effective leadership and did his best throughout his long career to meet those expectations. Providing inclusive, honest, results-oriented civic leadership will build trust, strengthen relationships, unleash your community's energy, and yield results long after you have left office.

notes

Chapter 1: Why We Did It

1. M. Magnet, "How Business Bosses Saved a Sick City," *Fortune*, March 27, 1989.

2. James E. Austin, "Business Leadership Lessons from the Cleveland Turnaround," *California Management Review* 41, no. 1 (Fall 1998): 86–106, 89.

3. Ed Richard, private correspondence.

4. Abraham Lincoln, "Fragment on Government, [July 1, 1854?]," in *The Collected Works of Abraham Lincoln*, ed. Roy P. Basler (New Brunswick, NJ: Rutgers University Press, 1953), 2:220–21.

5. All sums are denominated in dollar value at the time referenced.

6. Cleveland Foundation, *Cleveland Foundation 1978 Annual Report* (Cleveland, OH: Cleveland Foundation, 1978), 8.

7. Ed Richard, private correspondence.

8. Morton Mandel, interview, quoted in James E. Austin and Andrea L. Strimling, *The Cleveland Turnaround (A): Responding to the Crisis, 1978–88*, Harvard Business School Case Studies, no. 9-796-151 (Cambridge, MA: Harvard Business School, 1996), 5–6.

9. Jay Westbrook, private correspondence.

Chapter 2: The Cleveland Operations Improvement Task Force

1. The full final report can be found at Ohio, Operations Improvement Task Force, "City of Cleveland/Operations Improvement

Task Force Final Report, July 1980," *Voinovich Collections*, accessed May 2, 2017, http://www.voinovichcollections.library.ohio .edu/items/show/580.

2. The full report on implementation can be found at Ohio, Operations Improvement Task Force, "Operations Improvement Task Force Report on Implementation, ca. 1982," *Voinovich Collections*, accessed May 2, 2017, http://www.voinovichcollections .library.ohio.edu/items/show/579.

Chapter 3: The Audit

1. Although the firm has undergone many name changes over the years, I refer to it as "Deloitte" throughout.

2. Bill Reidy, private correspondence.

Chapter 4: The Cleveland OITF and Total Quality Management

1. Ken Myers, "Cleveland Pair Leave Their Mark," *USA Today*, December 28, 1989, 2A.

2. Tom Wagner, private correspondence.

3. W. Edwards Deming, Quality Services through Partnership summary, 1993.

4. Paul Goldberg, quoted in Ohio Office of Quality Services, *Ohio's Quality Journey*, brochure (Columbus: Ohio Office of Quality Services, 1997), 2.

Chapter 5: The Mayor's Operation Volunteer Effort and How to Sustain Your Gains

1. Morton Mandel, private correspondence.

Chapter 6: The Pivotal Role of Foundations

1. William Doll, "The Foundation and Municipal Governance: Helping the City Do Its Work," *Cleveland Foundation Perspective*, January 1966.

2. Cleveland Foundation, *Cleveland Foundation 1978 Annual Report* (Cleveland, OH: Cleveland Foundation, 1978), 8.

3. Nancy Humphrey, Peter M. Wilson, and George E. Peterson, *The Future of Cleveland's Capital Plant*, America's Urban Capital Stock (Washington, DC: Urban Institute, 1979).

4. David Abbott, private correspondence.

5. Robert Jaquay, *Civic Vision: Participatory City Planning in Cleveland in the 1980s*, Harvard Kennedy School Case Studies, no. C 16-91-1060.0 (Cambridge, MA: Harvard Kennedy School Case Program, 1991).

further reading

The following list is a brief overview of additional readings and resources reflecting current research and case studies of public-private partnerships.

Books

Delmon, Jeffrey. *Public-Private Partnership Projects in Infrastructure: An Essential Guide for Policy Makers*. Cambridge: Cambridge University Press, 2011.

> Delmon explains the expanding role of P3s in the efficient building of America's infrastructure.

Engel, Eduardo, Ronald D. Fischer, and Alexander Galetovic. *The Economics of Public-Private Partnerships: A Basic Guide*. Cambridge: Cambridge University Press, 2014.

> In recent years, governments have shifted toward the use of P3s to help with the construction and maintenance of infrastructure. This book addresses key issues, such as when governments should rely on P3s and how they should be implemented.

Wegrich, Kai, Genia Kostka, and Gerhard Hammerschmid, eds. *The Governance of Infrastructure*. 4th ed. Oxford: Oxford University Press, 2017.

> This book examines the decision-making process in infrastructure projects from sociological and public

administration points of view in addition to the usual political and economic analyses.

Yescombe, Edward R. *Public-Private Partnerships: Principles of Policy and Finance*. Oxford: Butterworth-Heinemann, 2011.

> This book explains the key policy issues and finance concepts associated with P3s and explains the optimal environment for P3 success.

Article

Vogelsang-Coombs, Vera, William M. Denihan, and Melanie F. Baur. "The Transformative Effect of Public-Private Partnerships: An Inside View of Good Government under Mayors Voinovich and Jackson." *Journal of Public and Nonprofit Affairs* 2, no. 2 (2016): 101–26.

> This article provides an excellent summary of Mayor George Voinovich's OITF, Mayor Frank Jackson's Operations Efficiency Task Force, and their lasting effects on the city of Cleveland.

Online Resources and Case Studies

Bipartisan Policy Center: Infrastructure Case Studies
https://bipartisanpolicy.org/infrastructure-case-studies/

> The BPC provides a list of analytical P3 infrastructure case studies from across the country.

Institute for Public-Private Partnerships
http://www.ip3.org/

> IP3 provides services to parties included in P3s and is a good starting point for research.

National Council for Public and Private Partnerships
http://www.ncppp.org/resources/case-studies/

> The NCPPP showcases P3 case studies from across the nation, including areas such as energy, technology, and infrastructure.

Further Reading

World Bank Group: Public-Private Partnership in Infrastructure
    Resource Center
    https://ppp.worldbank.org/public-private-partnership/

> The WBG has compiled P3 cases that can be searched
> by topic, sector, and location. This site contains infor-
> mation regarding P3 laws and examples of bidding docu-
> ments and risk matrices.

Burning the Cleveland debt notes, June 25, 1987.
Photo by Warner Thomas, Jr. By permission of the City of Cleveland

Janet Voinovich and George V. Voinovich, 1994.
*Photo by Greg Stevens & Associates. By permission of
the George V. Voinovich Trust*

about the author

George Victor Voinovich (1936–2016) was born in Cleveland, Ohio, as the oldest of six children. He earned a bachelor of arts degree in government from Ohio University in 1958 and a law degree from the Ohio State University in 1961. He married his wife, Janet, in 1962, and they had four children: George, Betsy, Peter, and Molly.

Voinovich began his political career in 1963 as an assistant attorney general for the state of Ohio. He then served as a member of the state House of Representatives from 1967 to 1971. From 1971 to 1976, he served as auditor of Cuyahoga County and from 1977 to 1978 as a member of the Cuyahoga County Board of Commissioners. In 1978, Voinovich was elected lieutenant governor on the ticket with James A. Rhodes.

In 1990, after three terms as mayor of Cleveland, Voinovich was elected as the sixty-fifth governor of Ohio and reelected in 1994 by the widest margin of victory for any Ohio governor of the twentieth century. In 1998, Voinovich successfully ran for the U.S. Senate seat vacated by the retirement of Senator John Glenn.

After two terms in the Senate, Voinovich retired in January 2011 and was named a senior fellow at Cleveland State University and a visiting professor at his namesake institution, the George V. Voinovich School of Leadership and Public Affairs at Ohio University. He remained active in mentorship and public service until he passed away in June 2016.

CPSIA information can be obtained
at www.ICGtesting.com
Printed in the USA
BVHW072021210120
569693BV00003B/13

9 780821 422663